# AUSTRALIAN ABORIGINENS

STEVEN FERRY

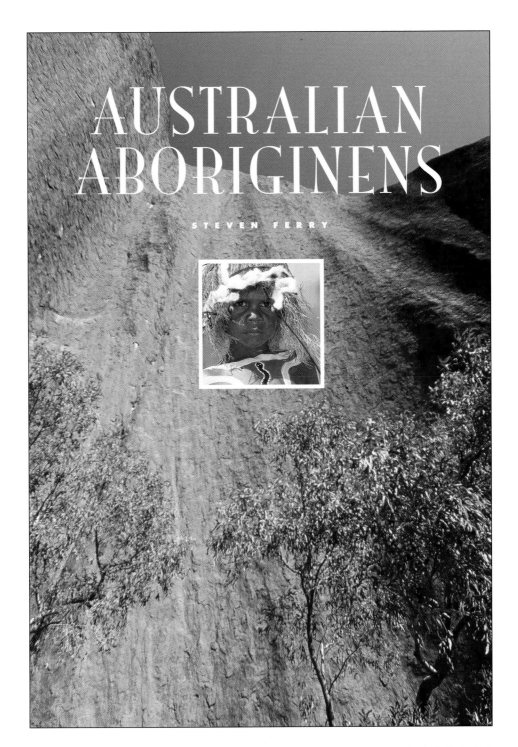

SMART APPLE MEDIA MANKATO MINNESOTA

Published by Smart Apple Media
123 South Broad Street, Mankato, Minnesota 56001

Produced by The Creative Spark, San Juan Capistrano, CA
    Editor: Elizabeth Sirimarco
    Designer: Mary Francis-DeMarois
    Art Direction: Robert Court
    Page Layout: Mary Francis-DeMarois

Photos/Illustrations: David Moore/Black Star/PNI 10, 17, 26;
Paul Chesley/Photographers/Aspen/PNI 4, 13; Kevin Davidson 8;
Paul Hurd/AllStock/PNI 11; Monkmeyer Press/Baglin 12, 18, 22, 24;
Monkmeyer Press/Rue 14, 20-21; Art Wolfe/AllStock/PNI 16;
Bob Race/Moon Publications, Inc. 23; Cary S. Wolinsky/Stock,
Boston/PNI 27; Paul Van Riel/Black Star/PNI 28

**Library of Congress Cataloging-in-Publication Data**
Ferry, Steven, 1953–
    Australian Aborigines / by Steven Ferry.
        p. cm. — (Endangered cultures)
    Includes bibliographical references and index.
    Summary: Details the origin, history, traditional way of life, and
religion of the aborigines of Australia, as well as their persecution,
current status, and struggle to preserve their culture and identity.
    ISBN 1-887068-73-2
    1. Australian aborigines—History—Juvenile literature. 2. Australian
aborigines—Social life and customs—Juvenile literature. [1. Australian
aborigines.] I. Title. II. Series.
GN666.F45  1999
944'.0049915—dc21                                        98-36421

First edition

9   8   7   6   5   4   3   2   1

# What Is an Australian Aborigine?

Aborigine is the English word for people who first inhabited, or are native to, a land before another group settled there. The word comes from the Latin language and means "from the beginning." Often the word is used to refer specifically to the native inhabitants of Australia.

Australia is both a country and a continent. It was first discovered by Europeans in 1530, but it was another 250 years, after an Englishman named Captain James Cook claimed Australia for England, before anyone but the Aborigines lived there.

No one knows for sure, but Australian Aborigines probably came to Australia from southern India tens of thousands of years ago. They traveled by rafts and canoes hollowed out of logs. The last ice age had lowered the sea levels, making the distances between Asia, Australia, and the islands in between them much shorter than they are today. Perhaps there was even a bridge of land that made traveling between the continents even easier. Aborigines

**50 MILLION YEARS AGO**

*Australia becomes an island.*

themselves do not believe that their ancestors immigrated to Australia. Instead, their tradition says that they have existed on the island since the time of creation.

Australia was once rich in forests and animal life, but many of the lakes and rivers dried up when the last ice age ended more than 20,000 years ago. The forests disappeared, leaving behind the hot, dry deserts that cover most of the island today. Even in such harsh conditions, the Aborigines—and a wide variety of wildlife—managed to adapt and survive.

Australia is home to most of the world's **marsupials,** animals that have an outside pouch where their young develop. North America, for example, has only one of these unusual creatures, the opossum. In Australia, most mammals are marsupials, including the kangaroo, wallaby, koala bear, and wombat.

The Aborigines were very much dependent on the island's animals for their survival. Aborigines ate a wide variety of prey, including bats, lizards, snakes (some as long as six feet), and frogs. They even ate insects, and with 50,000 different insect species (including the world's most poisonous spider), they found plenty that could be used for food.

Although Australia is about the same size as the contiguous, or connected, United States, the Australian population is much smaller, primarily because most of the island is too hot and dry for people to live comfortably.

The majority of Australians live along the eastern coast of the country in cities such as Sydney, Melbourne, and Brisbane. Aborigines, however, often live outside the major cities, in part because nature and the environment are important aspects of their culture. European settlers, who came to Australia only 200 years ago, preferred not to live with the Aborigines. So, the settlers forced them to leave the coastal regions that were the most desirable places to live. Although Aborigines once roamed the entire continent, today most live in the outback (the wild and remote regions of Australia) and on the outskirts of cities and towns.

100,000-40,000 B.C.

*Aborigines arrive in Australia.*

## AMAZING ANIMALS

Australia is filled with amazing animals. The kangaroo, for instance, can hop at speeds of 40 miles per hour in 12-foot bounds. The wombat is a 140-pound mole that makes the longest underground tunnels in the world. Koala bears, which are not bears at all, don't need to drink water to survive. In fact, koala means "no drink" in Aboriginal languages. They find all the liquid they need in the eucalyptus tree leaves they eat. The duckbill platypus is found only in Australia. It suckles its young, like a mammal; has webbed feet and a beak like a duck; and fur and claws like an otter. It closes its eyes and ears when underwater, using sonar to capture prey. Australia's waters are filled with unusual species as well. For the first six years of its life, the silver barramunda is a male fish—then it turns into a female!

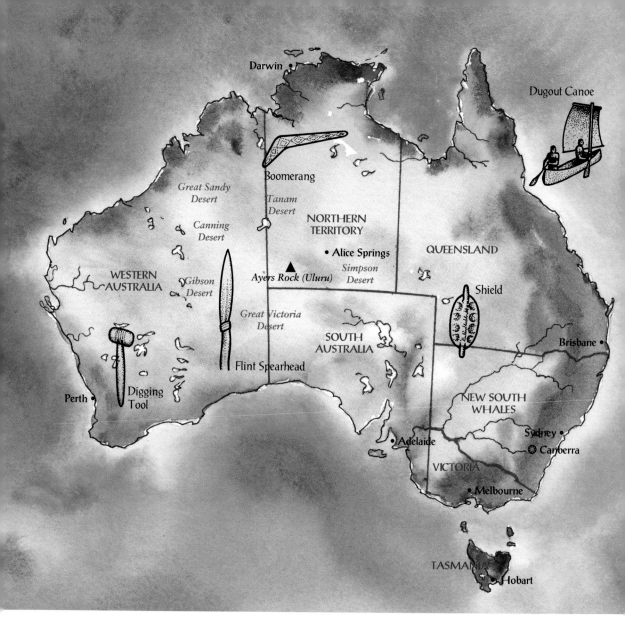

Darwin •

Dugout Canoe

*Great Sandy Desert*

*Tanam Desert*

Boomerang

NORTHERN TERRITORY

*Canning Desert*

• Alice Springs

QUEENSLAND

WESTERN AUSTRALIA

*Gibson Desert*

Ayers Rock (Uluru) ▲

*Simpson Desert*

Shield

*Great Victoria Desert*

SOUTH AUSTRALIA

Brisbane •

Flint Spearhead

Perth •

Digging Tool

NEW SOUTH WHALES

Adelaide •

Sydney •

Canberra

VICTORIA

• Melbourne

TASMANIA

Hobart •

Australia is almost the same size as the contiguous United States, but it has a population of only about 18.5 million, compared to more than 250 million in the U.S. Most Australians live on the eastern coast. Since the arrival of European settlers in 1788, Aborigines have been pushed ever farther from the mild climates of the coast. Today they live on the outskirts of big cities, as well as in the outback—the wild regions away from the settled areas of Australia. This map shows some traditional Aborigine tools and regions where they were frequently used.

# Boomerangs

Australian Aborigines invented boomerangs (curved throwing sticks) that return to the thrower. Less curved, non-returning boomerangs existed in ancient Egypt, Southern India, and California. Boomerangs are used for hunting, games, and war. They can be thrown directly at prey, or they are thrown like a baseball but downward. They immediately soar upward 100 yards (91 meters), making a circle before returning to the thrower. When thrown like this, they are used to imitate a hawk. A flock of birds will try to flee from "the hawk" and fly straight into the Aborigines' nets.

*An Aborigine prepares to throw his boomerang.*

To catch fish, they often used their bare hands, but spears, traps, and nets made of fiber and sewn with wooden needles were used as well. They also used fiber fishing line and hooks made from seashells. In just 30 minutes, they could make fishing canoes from tree bark, and these crafts would last for two years.

Emus and wallabies were caught by digging deep pits and covering them with leaves and brush so the animals fell into them. The Aborigines also ate moths and bees that, when roasted, tasted like sweet nuts.

Even with their excellent hunting skills, the Aborigine diet was mostly vegetarian and generally eaten raw. Berries, seeds, roots, pods, fruits, nuts, bulbs, vegetables, and honey

*This man, dressed for a traditional celebration, holds a* woomera, *an object that helps Aborigine hunters throw their spears farther.*

were all staples of their diet. Their knowledge of plants gave them many foods, as well as cosmetics and glues. Plants also provided medicines for everything from colds to poison **antidotes**. Some of these were similar to the remedies people use today.

Because Aborigines moved about so much, they had few possessions. The women carried all their belongings—such as digging sticks, wooden dishes, and food—in woven baskets. The men carried weapons for self-defense and hunting. Babies were tied on the mother's shoulders in cradles made from animal skins.

Aborigines did not live in houses, but during mosquito season, they built beehive-shaped huts of grass and bark and lit small fires inside them to keep the insects out. In windy areas, they might build a windbreak. In colder climates or seasons, they would use kangaroo or opossum skins sewn together or smear animal fat over their bodies to keep warm. Dingoes, native Australian dogs, were used for various purposes, including snuggling up with for warmth on cold nights.

**1770**

*Captain Cook lands in Eastern Australia and claims the country for England.*

*While many Aborigines dress and talk much like other Australians, they have very different traditions. Here two women hold an infant over a smoldering fire. "Baby smoking," as this practice is called, is an ancient rite of the Aborigine people, believed to protect an infant's health.*

13

*Ayers Rock, or Uluru, is the largest monolith (single rock) in the world, with most of it lying beneath the ground. Land is sacred to Australian Aborigines and is considered to be the source of life. Uluru is a place of great spiritual significance for many Aborigine groups.*

# Living
# Together

Australian Aborigines were divided into clans with common ancestors. These clans shared the same rituals, traditions, laws, and "churches" (areas that are spiritually important).

Clans were divided into smaller groups or families of 15 to 30 people. All the men in the group were called "father" by the children, and all the women "mother." The men might have three or four wives. Aborigines took good care of their children, as well as their elders. Life was very harsh, however, and they took some actions that seem cruel today. If a baby were born deformed, if the mother died, or if a baby were born too soon after another, the group would kill it. A mother could only look after one baby at a time, and they had no substitutes, such as cow's milk, to feed the baby if the mother died. Very old people, too, were killed when they could no longer keep up with the family.

While the Aborigines believed in their brotherhood with each other and with nature, they also had a darker side. They murdered members of other tribes to avenge the killing of

1788

*The first white
colony, a prison,
is established
on Australia.*

*A man teaches young Aborigine boys traditional carving techniques.*

one of their own family. Enemies from different clans lined up facing each other with 20 yards (18 meters) between them and threw spears. Many men died in this way. When people died from disease, the survivors might claim a neighboring tribe had cast a spell and attack them. Roughly one in 300 people died from revenge killings every year.

Nonetheless, the Aborigines generally lived peacefully together. While they usually stayed in their own territory, they might travel long distances for ceremonies or to trade with neighbors. Sometimes they exchanged gifts with friends and relatives in distant parts. They also met at certain times in places where fruit or animals were plentiful and used the time to feast on the ample food, swap stories, barter, and fight.

Young boys were taught everything by the men, and the girls by the women. Parents arranged the marriage of their daughter while she was still an infant. When boys were seven years old, they were taught to hunt and survive. They also had to learn tribal legends by heart. School was a raised circle of earth called a *burr-nong* ring.

**1819**

*A law is passed to remove part-Aborigine babies from their parents.*

*An Aborigine elder paints designs on the face and torso of a young boy. Makeup such as this was worn both in celebrations and when hunting.*

Corroborees *are celebrations, usually held at night, in which the Aborigines use dance and song to tell stories. Here, a man plays an instrument called a* didgeridoo.

# Spirits Among Us

Like Native Americans, the Australian Aborigines did not think that people could own land. The Earth was the physical side of the spiritual world and the sacred home of the Aborigines. They believed the Earth and its plants, animals, and people were all created long ago by spirits who took on human forms during **Dreamtime.**

During Dreamtime, the spirits taught man how to find food, perform ceremonies, dance, sing, paint, and enforce laws. At the end of Dreamtime, some of the spirits turned into the animals and birds. Others disappeared back into the Earth from which they came. These places were sacred Dreaming places. The Aborigines still believe that the spirits live at the special sites, and that their own souls go to such places when their bodies die. Even today, the men look after these Dreaming places, performing ceremonies to communicate with the Dreamtime spirits.

To the Aborigines, all life forms—including man—descend from these Dreamtime spirits and possess some of their energy. Aborigines often sang a magic song to make something mystical happen, such as healing a broken finger.

This photograph shows an "X-ray" painting, an ancient Aborigine art form in which the skeletons of animals were visible. Animals were of great spiritual importance to the Aborigines. Each clan had a sacred animal, the spirit of which gave the clan magical powers and skills. Clan members were not allowed to kill that animal.

*The last Tasmanian
Aborigine dies.*

*As with many cultures, the Aborigines use art to express spiritual ideas.
Here, two men display wooden carvings of spirits.*

Traditional stories were handed down from father to son, telling how the spirits made the world and continued to influence life. The stories were often acted out in long ceremonies called **corroborees,** in which the men painted their bodies with ochers and decorated themselves with emu feathers. The *corroborees* included music and dance, with hand clapping and "click sticks" to keep rhythm. Some tribes used a wind instrument called a **didgeridoo.** When something important happened, the Aborigines would meet and decide how it should be recorded in song and dance. Then the players learned and practiced their parts before performing the *corroboree.*

Aborigines also painted or carved images of the spirits on rock or wood. They then sang special words to persuade the spirit to enter the painting or carving. Paintings often showed the insides of animals, like X-rays.

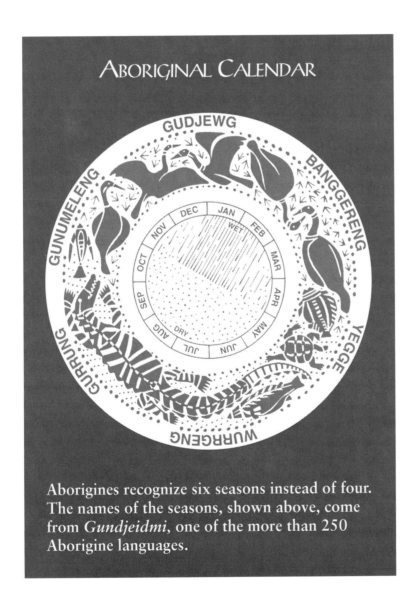

ABORIGINAL CALENDAR

Aborigines recognize six seasons instead of four. The names of the seasons, shown above, come from *Gundjeidmi*, one of the more than 250 Aborigine languages.

*A lone white child goes to class with Aborigine children. Since the arrival of European settlers more than 200 years ago, the Aborigines have been largely segregated, or kept apart, from other Australians.*

# Surviving
# with the
# White Man

When the English established their first Australian colony in 1788, there were probably about one million Aborigines living on the island, although there may have been as many as three million. These people lived in groups of 700 clans and spoke more than 250 different languages. Today there are only about 200,000 Aborigines left, of which only about 45,000 are full-blooded. Only 100 languages are still spoken, and two-thirds of all Aborigines no longer live in clans. So what happened?

Many Aborigines died from diseases the Europeans brought with them to Australia. Most settlers, however, thought of the Aborigines as savages whose lives had the same value as animals. As late as 1950, Aborigines were hunted illegally as a sport. When the Europeans wanted to raise sheep and mine minerals, they killed any Aborigines that got in their way. Settlers introduced cattle and sheep that destroyed the watering holes and the wildlife the Aborigines depended on. The Aborigines

*The Aborigines have a very different life than other Australians. Although Australia is a rich country, many Aborigines live in poverty similar to that in the poorest countries of the world.*

then killed the sheep and cattle for food and so were in turn killed by the ranchers. Some Aborigines worked hard on the settlers' ranches, receiving only food, tobacco, or clothing instead of pay.

It seems the settlers believed that the Aborigine "problem" would go away eventually when all the Aborigines finally died. In some places, they did: 4,000 Aborigines once lived on the island of Tasmania, south of Australia. The last of these people died in 1876.

Like the Native Americans, the Aborigines were removed from the lands they had inhabited for thousands of years and placed on **reservations.** They watched as settlers changed forever the sacred lands they once roamed. Christian missions were established to help them understand a "better" religion. Laws were passed, supposedly to assist the "inferior" race. In 1819, for instance, a law was passed that removed a child of mixed race (having one Aborigine and one white parent) from his or her parents to be brought up as a Christian.

In 1951, another law was passed that tried to force Australian Aborigines to give up their culture. They were brought into government settlements to teach them a new way of life. They were not allowed to move freely, own property, work certain jobs, or marry whom they wanted. The Aborigines, however, were not interested in living like the European settlers. They clung to their culture. Even the Aborigines who lived in big cities continued to speak their own languages, do things together, and enjoy traditional pastimes.

**1976**

*A law is passed recognizing that Aborigines are entitled to their lands.*

*A young Aborigine girl attends school in the city of Perth. Unfortunately, many Aborigine are still illiterate, unable to read or write.*

*Many people celebrated on "Australia Day" in 1988, which commemorated the arrival of European settlers to the island 200 years earlier. Aborigines protested the event. To them, the day marked the beginning of an era in which they became outsiders in their own homeland.*

In May 1967, Australian voters decided to allow Aborigines to become citizens, meaning they could vote and receive other benefits. The Department of Aboriginal Affairs was created to pass laws that would help the Aborigines. Five years later, another law granted the Aborigines the right to rule themselves on their own lands. Since then, they have been busy protecting their heritage, as well as their rights. Some sacred sites are now protected from mining or other development.

In the 1960s, one tribe demanded their land back. The government refused. When the Aborigines went to court to fight the government, the judge insisted no one had lived on the land before 1788, and therefore no one could claim it. The Aborigines persisted, and in 1976, a law was passed that recognized some of their claims. The Australian government is considering returning half of the Northern Territory to the Aborigines. In 1992, the highest court in Australia agreed that the Aborigines were the original "owners" of the land. Any existing owners, however, could also keep their land.

1992

*The highest court in Australia agrees that the Aborigines were the original "owners" of the land.*

Although aboriginal life has changed drastically over much of populated Australia, many Aborigines still live fairly traditional lives on reservations. Many who live in the outback do not speak English, while others have been taught both their own language and English. Some Aborigines speak **Kriol,** their own version of English.

While the white government has started to help Aborigines, there are still many problems after 200 years of mistreatment. Unemployment among Aborigines is four times the national average. One in four prisoners is an Aborigine, yet Aborigines make up less than two percent of the population. Aborigines can expect to live 20 years less than their white peers because health conditions are so bad on reservations. Some Aborigines have given up hope and taken to alcohol and drugs, so alcohol has been banned in many aboriginal communities. Because of all these difficulties, Aborigines are fighting for change, demanding better housing and health facilities for their people.

As Aborigines work to save their traditional way of life, they have also accepted their role in modern Australia, taking what they find useful, such as telephones, satellite television, and automobiles. At the same time, they have held on to their cultural identity through the many traditions of their people. Moving into the future, the story of the Aborigines is one of crisis and of hope.

# Glossary

**Aborigine**   The first people to inhabit any land. The term is often used more specifically to describe the first inhabitants of Australia.

**antidote**   A remedy to counteract the effects of a poison.

*corroboree*   Aborigine ceremonies or celebrations that include traditional dancing and singing.

*didgeridoo*   A wind instrument of the Australian Aborigines.

**Dreamtime**   The English word for the Aborigines' creation story.

**flush**   To cause prey, such as birds or animals, to suddenly fly or run from cover, making them easier to hunt.

**Kriol**   An Aborigine version of English.

**marsupials**   Animals in which the female has an outside pouch where its babies develop and nurse.

**ochers**   Red, yellow, or brown pigments used as paint. The Aborigines often used ochers to decorate the body.

**reservation**   Public land set aside for aboriginal people who have been removed from their homelands.

*woomera*   A two-foot long stick with a cup or hook at the end used to launch a spear.

# Further Reading and Information

BOOKS:

Johnson, Marael. *Outback Australia Handbook*. Chico, CA: Moon Publications, Inc., 1996.

Noonuccal, Oodgeroo. *Dreamtime: Aboriginal Stories*. New York, NY: Lothrop, Lee and Shepard Books, 1972.

WEB SITE:

http://www.abc.net.au/surf/explore/categ/indig.htm

# Index

**Items in bold print indicate illustration.**